GOD
Sees
HER

•———————•

40-Day
Devotional Journal

Our Daily Bread
Publishing.

HOW TO USE THIS BOOK

*T*he women writers of *Our Daily Bread* welcome you on an uplifting forty-day journey with the One who understands you perfectly, loves you unconditionally, and invites you into a love relationship with Him.

Through the *God Sees Her 40-Day Devotional Journal*, experience the profound comfort and joy of being in God's presence. You can trust that He sees you, that Jesus is intimately aware of—and will care for—your every need, and that His desires and purposes are for your good. During the next forty days, draw closer to God through

reading captivating, true-life stories in *God Hears Her* devotions;

connecting with Scripture through relevant Bible passages and journaling exercises; and

voicing your joys, fears, and disappointments to God through the guidance of prayer and journaling prompts.

As you come before God with vulnerability and trust, you'll discover that your beloved God longs to reciprocate: that Christ enters into your heartache and joys; that He desires to share His own griefs, sorrows, and delight; and that He wants to reveal His dreams and desires for you.

Whatever your circumstances, may you—during the next forty days of this journey—deepen your trust that God will revive your courage and awaken your faith.

Anna Haggard
General Editor

GENESIS 16:7–15

The angel of the LORD found Hagar near a spring in the desert; it was the spring that is beside the road to Shur. And he said, "Hagar, slave of Sarai, where have you come from, and where are you going?"

"I'm running away from my mistress Sarai," she answered.

Then the angel of the LORD told her, "Go back to your mistress and submit to her." The angel added, "I will increase your descendants so much that they will be too numerous to count."

The angel of the LORD also said to her:

> "You are now pregnant
> and you will give birth to a son.
> You shall name him Ishmael.
> for the LORD has heard of your misery.
> He will be a wild donkey of a man;
> his hand will be against everyone
> and everyone's hand against him,
> and he will live in hostility
> toward all his brothers."

She gave this name to the LORD who spoke to her: "You are the God who sees me," for she said, "I have now seen the One who sees me." That is why the well was called Beer Lahai Roi; it is still there, between Kadesh and Bered.

So Hagar bore Abram a son, and Abram gave the name Ishmael to the son she had borne.

I have God's full attention.

GOD SEES HER

My first eyeglasses opened my eyes to a bold world. Without glasses, items in the distance were a blur. At age twelve, with my first pair of eyeglasses, I was shocked to see clearer words on blackboards, tiny leaves on trees, and perhaps most important, big smiles on faces.

As friends smiled back when I greeted them, I learned that to be seen was as great a gift as the blessing of seeing.

The slave Hagar realized this as she fled from her mistress Sarai's unkindness. Hagar was a "nobody" in her culture, pregnant and alone, fleeing to a desert without help or hope. Seen by God, however, she was empowered to see Him. God became real to her—so real that she gave God a name, El Roi, which means, "You are the God who sees me." She said, "I have now seen the One who sees me" (Genesis 16:13).

Our God sees each of us too. Feeling unseen, alone, or like a nobody? God sees you and your future. In return, may we see in Him our ever-present hope, encouragement, salvation, and joy.

Patricia Raybon

Write

Do you find yourself in a wilderness season as Hagar was, in a time of abundance, or somewhere in-between? As you navigate this season, what do you want God to know?

She gave this name to the LORD who spoke to her: "You are the God who sees me," for she said, "I have now seen the One who sees me."

—GENESIS 16:13

Connect

Enter into Genesis 16:7–15 as Hagar. As you rest alongside the spring, take stock of your physical, mental, spiritual, and emotional health. Are you exhausted, fearful, hopeful? When you encounter the Stranger by the spring, what do you want to tell Him about where you've come from, and where you are going? How does it feel to be seen through His eyes of love and compassion?

Pray

At the start of this devotional journey, name a hope and a fear you're experiencing in this season. Talk with God about each.

MARK 12:38–44

As he taught, Jesus said, "Watch out for the teachers of the law. They like to walk around in flowing robes and be greeted with respect in the marketplaces, and have the most important seats in the synagogues and the places of honor at banquets. They devour widows' houses and for a show make lengthy prayers. These men will be punished most severely."

Jesus sat down opposite the place where the offerings were put and watched the crowd putting their money into the temple treasury. Many rich people threw in large amounts. But a poor widow came and put in two very small copper coins, worth only a few cents.

Calling his disciples to him, Jesus said, "Truly I tell you, this poor widow has put more into the treasury than all the others. They all gave out of their wealth; but she, out of her poverty, put in everything—all she had to live on."

People judge by outward appearances; Jesus looks at the heart.

PRICELESS WORSHIP

I use writing to worship and serve God, but when an acquaintance said he found no value in what I wrote, I became discouraged. I doubted the significance of my small offerings to God.

Through prayer, study of Scripture, and encouragement from my husband, the Lord affirmed that only He—not the opinions of other people—could determine our motives as a worshiper and the worth of our offerings to Him. I asked God to continue helping me develop skills and to provide opportunities to share the resources He gives me.

Jesus contradicted our standards of merit regarding our giving (Mark 12:41–44). While the rich tossed large amounts of money into the temple treasury, a poor widow put in coins "worth only a few cents" (v. 42). The Lord declared her gift to be greater than the rest (v. 43).

Every act of giving—not just financial—can be an expression of worship and loving obedience. When we present God the best of our time, talents, or treasure with hearts motivated by love, we are lavishing Him with offerings of priceless worship.

Xochitl Dixon

Pray

Identify one way you enjoy worshiping God. Ask
God how He feels when you praise Him.

Connect

The author writes that "Every act of giving—not just financial—can be an
expression of worship and loving obedience." Take an inventory of some of
the many ways you can worship God:

- Your time (commitments to church, family, work, dreams, hobbies)

....

....

- Your talents (job, creativity, gifts, skills, knowledge, expertise,
  connections)

....

....

- Your treasure (finances, non-financial giving)

....

....

Write

Where do you need courage to explore or press into a pursuit, gift, creative outlet, or challenge? As you journal about the situation, name your fears, desires, and excitement surrounding the possibility.

They all gave out of their wealth; but she, out of her poverty, put in everything—all she had to live on.

—MARK 12:44

PSALM 91 NLT

Those who live in the shelter of the
Most High
will find rest in the shadow of
the Almighty.
This I declare about the LORD:
He alone is my refuge, my place of
safety;
he is my God, and I trust him.
For he will rescue you from every
trap
and protect you from deadly
disease.
He will cover you with his feathers.
He will shelter you with his
wings.
His faithful promises are your
armor and protection.
Do not be afraid of the terrors of
the night,
nor the arrow that flies in the
day.
Do not dread the disease that stalks
in darkness,
nor the disaster that strikes at
midday.
Though a thousand fall at your side,
though ten thousand are dying
around you,
these evils will not touch you.
Just open your eyes,

and see how the wicked are
punished.

If you make the LORD your refuge,
if you make the Most High your
shelter,
no evil will conquer you;
no plague will come near your
home.
For he will order his angels
to protect you wherever you go.
They will hold you up with their
hands
so you won't even hurt your foot
on a stone.
You will trample upon lions and
cobras;
you will crush fierce lions and
serpents under your feet!

The LORD says, "I will rescue those
who love me.
I will protect those who trust in
my name.
When they call on me, I will
answer;
I will be with them in trouble.
I will rescue and honor them.
I will reward them with a long life
and give them my salvation."

God's comforting
presence provides safety
during life's storms.

PROMISE OF A PEACEFUL HOME

When I think of protection, I don't automatically think of a bird's feathers. Though a bird's feathers might seem like a flimsy form of protection, there is more to them than meets the eye.

Bird feathers are an amazing example of God's design. Feathers have a smooth part and a fluffy part. The smooth part has stiff barbs with tiny hooks that lock together like zipper prongs. The fluffy part keeps a bird warm. Together both parts of the feather protect the bird from wind and rain.

The image of God covering us with His feathers in Psalm 91:4 and other Bible passages (see Psalm 17:8) is one of comfort and protection. Like a parent whose arms are a safe place to retreat from a scary storm or a hurt, God's comforting presence provides safety and protection from life's emotional storms.

We can face trouble and heartache without fear as long as our faces are turned toward God. He is our refuge (91:2, 4, 9).

Linda Washington

He will cover you with his feathers.
He will shelter you with his wings. His
faithful promises are your armor and
protection. —PSALM 91:4 NLT

Write

Quiet yourself and listen to the comforting message of Psalm 91: "He will rescue you. . . . He will cover you with his feathers. He will shelter you with his wings. His faithful promises are your armor and protection" (vv. 3–4 NLT). What image from this passage do you need to hold on to today? Whatever image you choose, tuck it away in your mind as you go about your day, pulling it out often for strength and encouragement.

Connect

Identify one or more ways you have sought refuge in something apart from God

- in your job, relationship, or marital status;
- in your abilities, success, or achievements, whether in the community, at home, or at work;
- in your image, status, or popularity;
- in owning or acquiring things;
- in being seen as moral, wise, and just;
- in a social, religious, educational, or community group.

What have you learned from placing your ultimate hope in whatever you highlighted above?

Pray

Ask God to be your refuge in a current life storm,
and listen for His comfort and reassurance.

1 JOHN 4:7-16

Dear friends, let us love one another, for love comes from God. Everyone who loves has been born of God and knows God. Whoever does not love does not know God, because God is love. This is how God showed his love among us: He sent his one and only Son into the world that we might live through him. This is love: not that we loved God, but that he loved us and sent his Son as an atoning sacrifice for our sins. Dear friends, since God so loved us, we also ought to love one another. No one has ever seen God; but if we love one another, God lives in us and his love is made complete in us.

This is how we know that we live in him and he in us: He has given us of his Spirit. And we have seen and testify that the Father has sent his Son to be the Savior of the world. If anyone acknowledges that Jesus is the Son of God, God lives in them and they in God. And so we know and rely on the love God has for us.

God is love. Whoever lives in love lives in God, and God in them.

Though infinite, God's
love for me is personal.

JESUS LOVES MAYSEL

When my sister Maysel was little, she would sing a familiar song in her own way: "Jesus loves me, this I know, for the Bible tells Maysel." This irritated me to no end! As one of her older, "wiser" sisters, I knew the words were "me so," not "Maysel." Yet she persisted in singing it her way.

Now I think my sister had it right all along. The Bible does indeed tell Maysel, and all of us, that Jesus loves us. Take, for example, the writings of the apostle John, "the disciple whom Jesus loved" (John 21:7, 20). He tells us about God's love in one of the best-known verses of the Bible: John 3:16.

John reinforces that message of love in 1 John 4:10: "This is love: not that we loved God, but that he loved us and sent his Son as an atoning sacrifice for our sins." We too can have that same assurance: Jesus does love us. The Bible tells us so.

Alyson Kieda

Connect

Hear the apostle John's words about love: "Dear friends, since God so loved us, we also ought to love one another. No one has ever seen God; but if we love one another, God lives in us and his love is made complete in us. . . . God is love. Whoever lives in love lives in God, and God in them" (1 John 4:11–12, 16). Does a word, phrase, or sentence stand out to you? Write it down and reflect on the lessons it offers you.

Pray

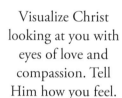

Visualize Christ looking at you with eyes of love and compassion. Tell Him how you feel.

Write

Confident in God's love for him, the apostle John called himself the "disciple whom Jesus loved" (John 21:7, 20). Write or speak to yourself, "I, [insert your name], am the disciple whom Jesus loves." How does it feel to identify yourself as Christ's beloved?

This is love: not that we loved God, but that he loved us and sent his Son as an atoning sacrifice for our sins. —1 JOHN 4:10

1 TIMOTHY 1:12–17 NLT

I thank Christ Jesus our Lord, who has given me strength to do his work. He considered me trustworthy and appointed me to serve him, even though I used to blaspheme the name of Christ. In my insolence, I persecuted his people. But God had mercy on me because I did it in ignorance and unbelief. Oh, how generous and gracious our Lord was! He filled me with the faith and love that come from Christ Jesus.

This is a trustworthy saying, and everyone should accept it: "Christ Jesus came into the world to save sinners"—and I am the worst of them all. But God had mercy on me so that Christ Jesus could use me as a prime example of his great patience with even the worst sinners. Then others will realize that they too can believe in him and receive eternal life. All honor and glory to God forever and ever! He is the eternal King, the unseen one who never dies; he alone is God. Amen.

My past mistakes don't
disqualify me from serving God.

MY REAL FACE

For years, I struggled with feelings of unworthiness and shame over my less-than-godly past. What if others found out?

One day God gave me the courage to invite a ministry leader to lunch. Striving for perfection, I scrubbed my house, whipped up a three-course meal, and donned my best jeans and blouse.

Rushing outside to turn off the sprinklers, I was drenched by a gush of water. With towel-dried hair and smeared makeup, I changed into dry sweatpants and a T-shirt . . . just as the doorbell rang. Frustrated, I confessed my morning's antics and motives. My new friend shared her own fear, insecurity, and guilt over lunch. After prayer, she welcomed me to her team of God's imperfect servants.

Accepting his new life in Christ, Paul refused to deny his past or let it stop him from serving (1 Timothy 1:12–14). He knew he had been saved and changed through Jesus's work on the cross. So Paul praised God and encouraged others to trust the Lord (vv. 15–17).

When we accept God's forgiveness, we're freed from our past. We have no reason to be ashamed of our real faces as we serve others.

Xochitl Dixon

The apostle Paul writes that God showed him mercy and immense patience (1 Timothy 1:16). How has God shown you mercy and patience?

I thank Christ Jesus our Lord, who has given me strength to do his work. He considered me trustworthy and appointed me to serve him.

—1 TIMOTHY 1:12 NLT

Connect

In 1 Timothy 1:12–17, Paul shares about his faith journey. Make a map of your own faith journey by journaling your testimony to God, noting significant people, events, and experiences with God. Describe the landscapes of your life (whether seasons of abundance and fruitfulness or of barren wilderness) along the way.

Pray

Identify where you struggle with unworthiness, shame, or insecurity. Let God show you how He sees you.

MATTHEW 14:25–33

Shortly before dawn Jesus went out to them, walking on the lake. When the disciples saw him walking on the lake, they were terrified. "It's a ghost," they said, and cried out in fear.

But Jesus immediately said to them: "Take courage! It is I. Don't be afraid."

"Lord, if it's you," Peter replied, "tell me to come to you on the water."

"Come," he said.

Then Peter got down out of the boat, walked on the water and came toward Jesus. But when he saw the wind, he was afraid and, beginning to sink, cried out, "Lord, save me!"

Immediately Jesus reached out his hand and caught him. "You of little faith," he said, "why did you doubt?"

And when they climbed into the boat, the wind died down. Then those who were in the boat worshiped him, saying, "Truly you are the Son of God."

God's presence enables me
to do the impossible.

. . . .

WALKING ON WATER

*D*uring an especially cold winter, I ventured out to Lake Michigan, the fifth largest lake in the world, to see it frozen over. Bundled up on the beach, I noticed that the water was frozen in waves, creating an icy masterpiece.

Because the water was frozen solid, I had the opportunity to "walk on water." I took the first few steps tentatively, fearful the ice wouldn't hold me. As I cautiously explored this unfamiliar terrain, I couldn't help but think of Jesus calling Peter out of the boat onto the Sea of Galilee.

When the disciples saw Jesus walking on the water, their response was fear. But Jesus responded, "Take courage! It is I. Don't be afraid" (Matthew 14:26–27). Peter overcame his fear and stepped out onto the water because he knew Jesus was present. When his courageous steps faltered, Peter cried out to Jesus. Jesus was still there, near enough to reach out His hand to rescue him.

If Jesus is calling you to do something that may seem as impossible as walking on water, take courage. The one who calls you will be present with you.

Lisa M. Samra

Pray

Identify something you'd like to do but fear
stepping out and doing; tell Jesus you need His
help to be courageous. What is Jesus's response?

Connect

Enter Matthew 14 as one of the disciples in the boat. Use your five senses to
immerse yourself in the sights, smells, sounds, feel, and tastes found in the
setting. As Christ walks on water, are you afraid, amazed, incredulous? What
is Jesus's invitation to you? What do you need from Jesus as you respond to
Him?

Write

What part of the scene from today's Bible story stands out to you? What about it draws you in?

Jesus immediately said to them: "Take courage! It is I. Don't be afraid."

—MATTHEW 14:27

LUKE 6:46–49 ESV

Why do you call me "Lord, Lord," and not do what I tell you? Everyone who comes to me and hears my words and does them, I will show you what he is like: he is like a man building a house, who dug deep and laid the foundation on the rock. And when a flood arose, the stream broke against that house and could not shake it, because it had been well built. But the one who hears and does not do them is like a man who built a house on the ground without a foundation. When the stream broke against it, immediately it fell, and the ruin of that house was great.

Peace can be found
through building my life
on Christ and His Word.

THE HOUSE ON THE ROCK

After living in their house for several years, my friends realized that their living room was sinking—cracks appeared on the walls and a window would no longer open. They learned that this room had been added without a foundation. Rectifying the shoddy workmanship would mean months of work as a new foundation was laid.

They had the work done, and when I visited them afterwards, I couldn't detect much difference. But I understood that a solid foundation matters.

This is true in our lives as well.

Jesus shared a parable about wise builders to illustrate the wisdom of listening to Him (Luke 6:46–49). Those who hear and obey His words are like the person who builds a house on a firm foundation. Jesus assured His listeners that when the storms come, their house would stand. Their faith would not be shaken.

We can find peace knowing that as we obey Jesus, He forms a strong foundation for our lives. Then when we face the torrents of rain lashing against us, we can trust that our foundation is solid. Our Savior will provide the support we need.

Amy Boucher Pye

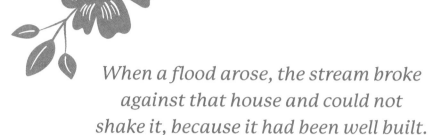

When a flood arose, the stream broke against that house and could not shake it, because it had been well built.

—LUKE 6:48 ESV

Write

Think about a time you built your life on something independent of Christ's ways and wisdom. How did that feel or turn out?

Connect

Slowly read the excerpt from today's Bible passage, noticing what word, phrase, or sentence stands out to you. What is Christ inviting you to do?

> Everyone who comes to me and hears my words and does them, I will show you what he is like: he is like a man building a house, who dug deep and laid the foundation on the rock. And when a flood arose, the stream broke against that house and could not shake it, because it had been well built. But the one who hears and does not do them is like a man who built a house on the ground without a foundation. When the stream broke against it, immediately it fell, and the ruin of that house was great. (Luke 6:47–49 ESV)

Pray

Identify an area of your life where you need peace, inner freedom, or encouragement. Bring it to God in prayer.

ISAIAH 44:21–23 NLT

"Pay attention, O Jacob,
    for you are my servant, O Israel.
I, the LORD, made you,
    and I will not forget you.
I have swept away your sins like a cloud.
    I have scattered your offenses like the morning mist.
Oh, return to me,
    for I have paid the price to set you free."

Sing, O heavens, for the LORD has done this
       wondrous thing.
    Shout for joy, O depths of the earth!
Break into song,
    O mountains and forests and every tree!
For the LORD has redeemed Jacob
    and is glorified in Israel.

Jesus promises never to remember my sins.

SWEPT AWAY

When he invented the pencil eraser in 1770, British engineer Edward Nairne was reaching for a piece of bread. Crusts of bread were used then to erase marks on paper. Picking up a piece of latex rubber by mistake, Nairne found it erased his error, leaving rubberized "crumbs" easily swept away by hand.

Our sins—our worst errors—can be swept away. It's the Lord—the Bread of Life—who cleans them with His own life, promising never to remember our sins.

This can seem to be a remarkable fix—and not deserved. For many, it's hard to believe our past sins can be swept away by God "like the morning mist" (Isaiah 44:22 NLT). Does God, who knows everything, forget them so easily?

That's exactly what God does when we accept Jesus as our Savior. Choosing to forgive our sins and to remember them no more, our heavenly Father frees us to move forward (Jeremiah 31:34).

Yes, consequences may remain. But God sweeps sin itself away, inviting us to return to Him for our clean new life. There's no better way to be swept away.

Patricia Raybon

Connect

Where are you captive to a destructive habit, addiction, or negative thought pattern? Invite Jesus to take a look along with you. Ask your compassionate Savior for freedom from your bondage and shame.

Pray

Take time to thank God for having swept away your sins "like the morning mist" (Isaiah 44:22 NLT).

Write

In what area of your life have you have experienced God's forgiveness and a chance to start anew?

I have swept away your sins like a cloud.
I have scattered your offenses like the
morning mist. —ISAIAH 44:22 NLT

2 KINGS 19:9–19 ESV

Now the king heard concerning Tirhakah king of Cush, "Behold, he has set out to fight against you." So he sent messengers again to Hezekiah, saying, "Thus shall you speak to Hezekiah king of Judah: 'Do not let your God in whom you trust deceive you by promising that Jerusalem will not be given into the hand of the king of Assyria. Behold, you have heard what the kings of Assyria have done to all lands, devoting them to destruction. And shall you be delivered? Have the gods of the nations delivered them, the nations that my fathers destroyed, Gozan, Haran, Rezeph, and the people of Eden who were in Telassar? Where is the king of Hamath, the king of Arpad, the king of the city of Sepharvaim, the king of Hena, or the king of Ivvah?'"

Hezekiah received the letter from the hand of the messengers and read it; and Hezekiah went up to the house of the LORD and spread it before the LORD. And Hezekiah prayed before the LORD and said: "O LORD, the God of Israel, enthroned above the cherubim, you are the God, you alone, of all the kingdoms of the earth; you have made heaven and earth. Incline your ear, O LORD, and hear; open your eyes, O LORD, and see; and hear the words of Sennacherib, which he has sent to mock the living God. Truly, O LORD, the kings of Assyria have laid waste the nations and their lands and have cast their gods into the fire, for they were not gods, but the work of men's hands, wood and stone. Therefore they were destroyed. So now, O LORD our God, save us, please, from his hand, that all the kingdoms of the earth may know that you, O LORD, are God alone."

> Whatever the challenge, I
> can run straight to God.

GIVE IT TO GOD

As a teenager, when I became overwhelmed by enormous challenges or high-stakes decisions, my mother taught me the merits of putting pen to paper to gain perspective. She taught me to write out the basic facts and possible actions with their likely outcomes. Then I could step back from the problem and view it more objectively.

Similarly, pouring our hearts out to God in prayer helps us gain His perspective and reminds us of His power. King Hezekiah did just that after receiving a daunting letter from an ominous adversary. The Assyrians threatened to destroy Jerusalem as they had many other nations. Hezekiah spread out the letter before the Lord, prayerfully calling on Him to deliver the people so that the world would recognize He alone is God (2 Kings 19:19).

When we're faced with a situation that brings anxiety, fear, or an awareness that it's more than we can handle, like Hezekiah let's run straight to the Lord. We too can lay our problem before God and trust Him to guide our steps and calm our uneasy hearts.

Kirsten Holmberg

Write

Are you making a decision or worrying about a challenging circumstance? Journal about the basic facts of your situation, outlining your possible actions with their possible outcomes. Review your findings with God, asking Him for direction and guidance about how to proceed wisely.

Hezekiah received the letter from the hand of the messengers and read it; and Hezekiah went up to the house of the Lord and spread it before the Lord.

—2 KINGS 19:14 ESV

Connect

Identify a circumstance that seems impossible to face on your own. In your mind's eye, visualize the setting—the who, what, when, and where. Now, imagine Jesus is physically present in that space. Feel His reassuring presence. Where is He in the scene? How does He respond to you with love and attentive care? Ask Him for what you need to take the next step.

Pray

Take inventory of your anxieties and concerns, and offer them to Jesus in prayer, trusting that He cares for you.

MATTHEW 11:25-30

At that time Jesus said, "I praise you, Father, Lord of heaven and earth, because you have hidden these things from the wise and learned, and revealed them to little children. Yes, Father, for this is what you were pleased to do.

"All things have been committed to me by my Father. No one knows the Son except the Father, and no one knows the Father except the Son and those to whom the Son chooses to reveal him.

"Come to me, all you who are weary and burdened, and I will give you rest. Take my yoke upon you and learn from me, for I am gentle and humble in heart, and you will find rest for your souls. For my yoke is easy and my burden is light."

> In following Jesus, I experience
> the rest I long for.

FREE TO FOLLOW

*M*y high school cross-country coach once advised me before a race, "Don't try to be in the lead. The leaders almost always burn out too quickly."

Leading can be exhausting; following can be freeing. Knowing this improved my running, but it took me a lot longer to realize how this applies to Christian discipleship. In my own life, I was prone to think being a believer in Jesus meant trying *really hard.* By pursuing my own exhausting expectations for what a Christian should be, I was inadvertently missing the joy and freedom found in simply following Him (John 8:32, 36).

Jesus promised that in seeking Him we will find the rest we long for (Matthew 11:25–28). Unlike many other religious teachers' emphasis on rigorous study of Scripture or an elaborate set of rules, Jesus taught that it's simply through knowing Him that we know God (v. 27). In seeking Him, we find our heavy burdens lifted (vv. 28–30) and our lives transformed.

Following Him, our gentle and humble Leader (v. 29), is never burdensome—it's the way of hope and healing. Resting in His love, we are free.

Monica La Rose

Pray

Talk with God about an area of your
life where you need rest.

Connect

Hear these words from Christ: "Come to me, all you who are weary and burdened, and I will give you rest. Take my yoke upon you and learn from me, for I am gentle and humble in heart, and you will find rest for your souls. For my yoke is easy and my burden is light" (Matthew 11:28–30). Identify a word, phrase, or sentence that comforts, challenges, or strikes you. Write it down, and ponder it as you go about your day.

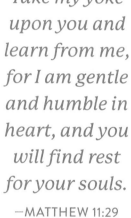

Write

Devotional author Monica La Rose writes that previously she thought following Jesus meant "trying *really hard*." How are you trying *really hard* to live up to your expectations of what a Christian should be?

Take my yoke upon you and learn from me, for I am gentle and humble in heart, and you will find rest for your souls.

—MATTHEW 11:29

ECCLESIASTES 3:9–13

What do workers gain from their toil? I have seen the burden God has laid on the human race. He has made everything beautiful in its time. He has also set eternity in the human heart; yet no one can fathom what God has done from beginning to end. I know that there is nothing better for people than to be happy and to do good while they live. That each of them may eat and drink, and find satisfaction in all their toil—this is the gift of God.

> Beauty gives me a glimpse
> of God's glory.

. . . .

ENJOYING BEAUTY

*T*he painting caught my eye like a beacon. Displayed on the wall of a long hospital hallway, its deep pastel hues and Navajo Native American figures were so arresting I stopped to marvel and stare.

"Beautiful," I whispered.

Many things in life are beautiful indeed. Master paintings. Scenic vistas. Inspired crafts. But so is a child's smile. A friend's hello. A robin's blue egg. A seashell's strong ridges. God "has made everything beautiful in its time" (Ecclesiastes 3:11). In such beauty, Bible scholars explain, we get a glimpse of the perfection of God's creation—including the glory of His perfect rule to come.

Some days life looks drab and futile. But God mercifully provides moments of beauty to ponder.

The artist of the painting I admired, Gerard Curtis Delano, understood that. "God [gave] me a talent to create beauty," he once said, "and this is what He wanted me to do."

Seeing such beauty, how can we respond? We can thank God for eternity to come while pausing to enjoy the glory we already see.

Patricia Raybon

He has made everything beautiful
in its time. —ECCLESIASTES 3:11

Write

In ancient cultures, the timing of things, actions, and events was significant. How have you seen the importance of timing in your own life and in the lives of others?

Connect

Artist Gerard Curtis Delano said, "God [gave] me a talent to create beauty . . . and this is what He wanted me to do." Even if you're not artistic in the traditional sense, you—being made in the image of your Creator—have gifts and talents to create order, beauty, and structure in the world around you. Write down your strengths and gifts and thank God for them.

Pray

Identify something beautiful that gives
you joy and thank God for it.

ISAIAH 35 ESV

The wilderness and the dry land
  shall be glad;
    the desert shall rejoice and
    blossom like the crocus;
it shall blossom abundantly
    and rejoice with joy and singing.
The glory of Lebanon shall be given
    to it,
    the majesty of Carmel and
    Sharon.
They shall see the glory of the
    LORD,
    the majesty of our God.

Strengthen the weak hands,
    and make firm the feeble knees.
Say to those who have an anxious
    heart,
    "Be strong; fear not!
Behold, your God
    will come with vengeance,
with the recompense of God.
    He will come and save you."

Then the eyes of the blind shall be
    opened,
    and the ears of the deaf
    unstopped;
then shall the lame man leap like a
    deer,
    and the tongue of the mute sing
    for joy.
For waters break forth in the
    wilderness,
    and streams in the desert;

the burning sand shall become a
    pool,
    and the thirsty ground springs of
    water;
in the haunt of jackals, where they
    lie down,
    the grass shall become reeds and
    rushes.

And a highway shall be there,
    and it shall be called the Way of
    Holiness;
the unclean shall not pass over it.
    It shall belong to those who walk
    on the way;
    even if they are fools, they shall
    not go astray.
No lion shall be there,
    nor shall any ravenous beast
    come up on it;
they shall not be found there,
    but the redeemed shall walk
    there.
And the ransomed of the LORD
    shall return
    and come to Zion with singing;
everlasting joy shall be upon their
    heads;
    they shall obtain gladness and
    joy,
    and sorrow and sighing shall flee
    away.

*Even barren places in my
life can produce fruit.*

BLOOMING IN
THE DESERT

The Mojave Desert includes the expected sand dunes, dry canyons, mesas, and mountains of most deserts. But American biologist Edmund Jaeger observed that every few years an abundance of rain results in "such a wealth of blossoms that almost every foot of sand or gravelly soil is hidden beneath a blanket of flowers." Researchers confirm that the dry earth needs to be soaked by storms and warmed by the sun, at just the right times, before blooms will cover the desert with vibrant colors.

This image of God bringing forth life despite the arid terrain reminds me of the prophet Isaiah. He shared an encouraging vison of hope after delivering God's message of judgment on all nations (Isaiah 35). Describing a future time when God will make all things right, the prophet said, "The wilderness and the dry land shall be glad; the desert shall rejoice and blossom" (v. 1 ESV). God's rescued people would enter His kingdom "with singing; everlasting joy shall be upon their heads" (v. 10 ESV).

Deeply rooted in God's love, we can grow, blooming into His likeness until, at just the right time, Jesus returns and sets all things right.

Xochitl Dixon

Connect

Reread Isaiah 35 and choose an image that is life-giving to you. What about it gives you hope, joy, or peace?

Pray

Have a conversation with God about something in your life that has been restored.

Write

Where in your life are you still waiting for hope and healing?

They shall see the glory of the LORD, the majesty of our God. —ISAIAH 35:2 ESV

EXODUS 33:18–19; 34:1–7

Then Moses said, "Now show me your glory."

And the LORD said, "I will cause all my goodness to pass in front of you, and I will proclaim my name, the LORD, in your presence. I will have mercy on whom I will have mercy, and I will have compassion on whom I will have compassion. . . ."

The LORD said to Moses, "Chisel out two stone tablets like the first ones, and I will write on them the words that were on the first tablets, which you broke. Be ready in the morning, and then come up on Mount Sinai. Present yourself to me there on top of the mountain. No one is to come with you or be seen anywhere on the mountain; not even the flocks and herds may graze in front of the mountain."

So Moses chiseled out two stone tablets like the first ones and went up Mount Sinai early in the morning, as the LORD had commanded him; and he carried the two stone tablets in his hands. Then the LORD came down in the cloud and stood there with him and proclaimed his name, the LORD. And he passed in front of Moses, proclaiming, "The LORD, the LORD, the compassionate and gracious God, slow to anger, abounding in love and faithfulness, maintaining love to thousands, and forgiving wickedness, rebellion and sin. Yet he does not leave the guilty unpunished; he punishes the children and their children for the sin of the parents to the third and fourth generation."

God is patient and kind.

. . . .

AN ANGRY GOD?

When I studied Greek and Roman mythology in college, I was struck by how easily angered the mythological gods were in the stories. The people on the receiving end of their anger found their lives destroyed, sometimes on a whim.

I was quick to scoff, wondering how anyone could believe in gods like that. But then I asked myself, Is my view of the God who actually exists much different? Don't I view Him as easily angered whenever I doubt Him? Sadly, yes.

That's why I appreciate Moses's request of God to "show me your glory" (Exodus 33:18). Having been chosen to lead people who often grumbled against him, Moses wanted to know that God would indeed help him. Moses's request was rewarded by a demonstration of God's glory. God announced to Moses His name and characteristics. He is "the compassionate and gracious God, slow to anger, abounding in love and faithfulness" (34:6).

We can see God and His glory in His patience with us, the encouraging word of a friend, a beautiful sunset, or—best of all—the whisper of God's grace inside of us.

Linda Washington

Write

God described Himself in Exodus 34:6 as compassionate, gracious, slow to anger, loving, and faithful. Identify one characteristic of God that stands out to you. How has God demonstrated this character trait in your relationship with Him?

The LORD, the LORD, the compassionate and gracious God, slow to anger, abounding in love and faithfulness.

—EXODUS 34:6

Connect

What does your heavenly Father look like to you? In your imagination, visualize God the Father. In relation to Him, are you close by or far away? Describe the setting. How does your heavenly Father engage with you—is He happy, sad, pleased, angry, or something else? As you journal about this experience, does anything surprising come up about your image of your heavenly Father?

Pray

Tell your heavenly Father how much you love
Him. How does God respond to you?

JONAH 2 NLT

Then Jonah prayed to the LORD his God from inside the fish. He said,

"I cried out to the LORD in my great trouble,
    and he answered me.
I called to you from the land of the dead,
    and LORD, you heard me!
You threw me into the ocean depths,
    and I sank down to the heart of the sea.
The mighty waters engulfed me;
    I was buried beneath your wild and stormy waves.
Then I said, 'O LORD, you have driven me from
        your presence.
    Yet I will look once more toward your holy Temple.'

"I sank beneath the waves,
    and the waters closed over me.
    Seaweed wrapped itself around my head.
I sank down to the very roots of the mountains.
    I was imprisoned in the earth,
    whose gates lock shut forever.
But you, O LORD my God,
    snatched me from the jaws of death!
As my life was slipping away,
    I remembered the LORD.
And my earnest prayer went out to you
    in your holy Temple.
Those who worship false gods
    turn their backs on all God's mercies.
But I will offer sacrifices to you with songs of praise,
    and I will fulfill all my vows.
    For my salvation comes from the LORD alone."

Then the LORD ordered the fish to spit Jonah out onto the beach.

Even when I run, God
pursues me in love.

UP A TREE

When my mother discovered my kitten, Velvet, devouring her homemade bread, she scooted the feline out the door. Later, as we searched for the missing cat, a faint meow whistled on the wind. I looked up to the peak of a poplar tree where a black smudge tilted a branch.

In her haste to flee my mother's frustration, Velvet chose a more precarious predicament. Is it possible that we sometimes do something similar—running from our errors and putting ourselves in danger? Even then, God comes to our rescue.

The prophet Jonah fled in disobedience from God's call to preach to Nineveh, and he was swallowed up by a great fish. "Then Jonah prayed to the LORD his God from inside the fish" (Jonah 2:1 NLT). God heard Jonah's plea, and the fish expelled the prophet (v. 10). Then God gave Jonah another chance (3:1).

After we failed to woo Velvet down, we summoned the fire department. A kind man climbed a ladder, plucked my kitten from her perch, and returned her safely to my arms.

Oh the heights—and the depths—God goes to in rescuing us from our disobedience with His redeeming love!

Elisa Morgan

Pray

Where in your life do you need a second
chance? Talk with God about it.

Connect

Where have you run from God, yourself, or others? How have you experienced God's relentless love in the face of your wandering, fear, or shame?

Write

Think about a time you were given a second chance.

I cried out to the LORD in my great trouble, and he answered me.

—JONAH 2:2 NLT

PSALM 33:6-19

By the word of the LORD the heavens were made,
    their starry host by the breath of his mouth.
He gathers the waters of the sea into jars;
    he puts the deep into storehouses.
Let all the earth fear the LORD;
    let all the people of the world revere him.
For he spoke, and it came to be;
    he commanded, and it stood firm.

The LORD foils the plans of the nations;
    he thwarts the purposes of the peoples.
But the plans of the LORD stand firm forever,
    the purposes of his heart through all generations.

Blessed is the nation whose God is the LORD,
    the people he chose for his inheritance.
From heaven the LORD looks down
    and sees all mankind;
from his dwelling place he watches
    all who live on earth—
he who forms the hearts of all,
    who considers everything they do.

No king is saved by the size of his army;
    no warrior escapes by his great strength.
A horse is a vain hope for deliverance;
    despite all its great strength it cannot save.
But the eyes of the LORD are on those who fear him,
    on those whose hope is in his unfailing love,
to deliver them from death
    and keep them alive in famine.

God's my attentive,
loving Father.

EYES IN THE BACK OF MY HEAD

I was mischievous in my early years and tried to hide my bad behavior to avoid getting into trouble. Yet my mother usually found out what I had done. I recall being amazed at how accurately she knew about my antics. When I asked how she knew, she replied, "I have eyes in the back of my head." This, of course, led me to study her head whenever she'd turn her back—were the eyes invisible or merely cloaked by her red hair? Eventually I gave up looking for her extra pair of eyes and realized I just wasn't as sneaky as I thought. Her watchful gaze was evidence of her loving concern for us.

As grateful as I am for my mother's attentive care, I'm even more grateful that God "sees all mankind" (Psalm 33:13). He sees so much more than what we do; He sees our sadness, our delights, and our love for one another.

God sees our true character and always knows what we need. With perfect vision, He watches over those who love Him and put their hope in Him (v. 18). He's our attentive, loving Father.

Kirsten Holmberg

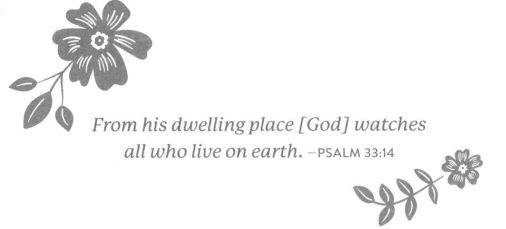

*From his dwelling place [God] watches
all who live on earth.* —PSALM 33:14

Write

Identify and reflect on a time God demonstrated His loving faithfulness to you.

Connect

Author Kirsten Holmberg writes, "With perfect vision, [God] watches over those who love Him and put their hope in Him (v. 18). He's our attentive, loving Father." How have you experienced God's watchful, personal care?

Pray

Where in your life are you having difficulty trusting God to provide for you? Tell God these frustrations and fears.

MATTHEW 25:31–40 NLT

But when the Son of Man comes in his glory, and all the angels with him, then he will sit upon his glorious throne. All the nations will be gathered in his presence, and he will separate the people as a shepherd separates the sheep from the goats. He will place the sheep at his right hand and the goats at his left.

Then the King will say to those on his right, "Come, you who are blessed by my Father, inherit the Kingdom prepared for you from the creation of the world. For I was hungry, and you fed me. I was thirsty, and you gave me a drink. I was a stranger, and you invited me into your home. I was naked, and you gave me clothing. I was sick, and you cared for me. I was in prison, and you visited me."

Then these righteous ones will reply, "Lord, when did we ever see you hungry and feed you? Or thirsty and give you something to drink? Or a stranger and show you hospitality? Or naked and give you clothing? When did we ever see you sick or in prison and visit you?"

And the King will say, "I tell you the truth, when you did it to one of the least of these my brothers and sisters, you were doing it to me!"

> Whenever I humbly serve
> others, I serve Christ.

JESUS IN DISGUISE

When a friend cared for her housebound mother-in-law, she asked her what she longed for the most. "For my feet to be washed," she replied. My friend told me, "How I hated that job! Each time she asked me to do it, I was resentful and would ask God to hide my feelings from her."

But one day her grumbling attitude changed in a flash. As she got out the bowl and towel and knelt at her mother-in-law's feet, she said, "I looked up, and for a moment I felt like I was washing the feet of Jesus himself. She was Jesus in disguise!" After that, she felt honored to do it.

When I heard this moving account, I thought of Jesus's story about the end of time, which He taught on the Mount of Olives. The King welcomes His sons and daughters into His kingdom, saying that when they visited the sick or fed the hungry, they did it for Him (Matthew 25:40). We, too, serve Jesus Himself when we visit those in prison or give clothes to the needy.

Today, might you echo my friend, who now wonders when she meets someone new, "Are you Jesus in disguise?"

Amy Boucher Pye

Connect

Author Amy Boucher Pye recounts the story of a friend who felt uncomfortable in completing her act of service until she recognized that it also honored Christ. Identify a routine task, chore, or service that is burdensome to you, and ask God for His perspective on your work.

Pray

Identify someone who may have been "Jesus in disguise" to you. Thank God for them.

Write

How have you served others? How might Christ be inviting you to serve?

The King will say, "I tell you the truth,
when you did it to one of the least of
these my brothers and sisters, you were
doing it to me!" —MATTHEW 25:40 NLT

LUKE 23:44–49

It was now about noon, and darkness came over the whole land until three in the afternoon, for the sun stopped shining. And the curtain of the temple was torn in two. Jesus called out with a loud voice, "Father, into your hands I commit my spirit." When he had said this, he breathed his last.

The centurion, seeing what had happened, praised God and said, "Surely this was a righteous man." When all the people who had gathered to witness this sight saw what took place, they beat their breasts and went away. But all those who knew him, including the women who had followed him from Galilee, stood at a distance, watching these things.

> May I never forget Christ's
> unspeakable sacrificial
> love on the cross.

LOOK AND BE QUIET

*I*n the song "Look at Him," Mexican composer Rubén Sotelo describes Jesus at the cross. He invites us to look at Jesus and be quiet, because there is really nothing to say before the type of love Jesus demonstrated at the cross.

When Jesus breathed His last, those who "had gathered to witness this sight . . . beat their breasts and went away" (Luke 23:48). Others stood at a distance (v. 49). They looked and were quiet. Only one spoke, a centurion, who said, "Surely this was a righteous man" (v. 47).

Many years before, Jeremiah wrote about Jerusalem's pain after its devastation. "Is it nothing to you, all you who pass by?" (Lamentations 1:12). He was asking people to look and see; he thought there was no greater suffering than Jerusalem's. However, has there been any suffering like Jesus's suffering?

All of us are passing by the road of the cross. Will we look and see His love? Let us take a moment to ponder Jesus's death. In the quietness of our hearts, may we whisper to Him our deepest devotion.

Keila Ochoa

Write

In Luke 23:46, Jesus said with absolute trust to His Father, "Father, into your hands I commit my spirit." Entrust to God whatever situation you're up against by journaling Christ's words: "Father, into your hands, I commit [this situation, this fear, this relationship . . .]." What are your thoughts and feelings as you release your request into God's hands? Listen for God's reply.

Look around and see. Is any suffering like my suffering?

—LAMENTATIONS 1:12

Connect

Visualize that you are on the road of the cross. Imagine you are in the story of Jesus's crucifixion, as either a disciple or a bystander. Look up at Jesus. Lock eyes with the suffering Servant who sacrificed it all so that you might be set free and made whole. Feel the depth of His love for you. In that moment, what do you want Him to know?

Pray

Tell Jesus what His sacrifice means to you.

LUKE 12:22–34 NLT

Then, turning to his disciples, Jesus said, "That is why I tell you not to worry about everyday life—whether you have enough food to eat or enough clothes to wear. For life is more than food, and your body more than clothing. Look at the ravens. They don't plant or harvest or store food in barns, for God feeds them. And you are far more valuable to him than any birds! Can all your worries add a single moment to your life? And if worry can't accomplish a little thing like that, what's the use of worrying over bigger things?

"Look at the lilies and how they grow. They don't work or make their clothing, yet Solomon in all his glory was not dressed as beautifully as they are. And if God cares so wonderfully for flowers that are here today and thrown into the fire tomorrow, he will certainly care for you. Why do you have so little faith?

"And don't be concerned about what to eat and what to drink. Don't worry about such things. These things dominate the thoughts of unbelievers all over the world, but your Father already knows your needs. Seek the Kingdom of God above all else, and he will give you everything you need.

"So don't be afraid, little flock. For it gives your Father great happiness to give you the Kingdom.

"Sell your possessions and give to those in need. This will store up treasure for you in heaven! And the purses of heaven never get old or develop holes. Your treasure will be safe; no thief can steal it and no moth can destroy it. Wherever your treasure is, there the desires of your heart will also be."

The secret to an abundant life
is having a right relationship
with God and others.

THE POINT OF BEING ALIVE

hile almost all financial advice books I've read imply that the primary reason to cut costs is to live like millionaires later, one book offered a refreshingly different perspective. It said living simply is essential for a rich life. If you need more stuff to feel joy, the book suggested, "You're missing the point of being alive."

That idea brought to mind Jesus's response when a man asked Him to urge his brother to divide an inheritance with him. Instead of sympathizing, Jesus warned him sternly about "all kinds of greed"—because "life does not consist in an abundance of possessions" (Luke 12:14–15). He then came to a blistering conclusion about this wealthy person's plans to store his crops and enjoy a luxurious lifestyle. His wealth did him no good, since he died that night (vv. 16–20).

Jesus's words remind us to check our motivation. Our hearts should be focused on pursuing God's kingdom—not just on securing our own futures (vv. 29–31). As we live for Him and freely share with others, we can fully enjoy a rich life with Him now (vv. 32–34).

Monica La Rose

Pray

Talk with God about the things you most treasure.

Connect

Reread Luke 12:22–34, then take inventory of the things you believe are essential for a truly rich life.

Does your lifestyle include what you identified will make your life full and abundant? If not, what might need to change?

Write

Identify one practice of living simply that gives you joy.

Wherever your treasure is, there the desires of your heart will also be.

—LUKE 12:34 NLT

NEHEMIAH 1 NLT

These are the memoirs of Nehemiah son of Hacaliah.

In late autumn, in the month of Kislev, in the twentieth year of King Artaxerxes' reign, I was at the fortress of Susa. Hanani, one of my brothers, came to visit me with some other men who had just arrived from Judah. I asked them about the Jews who had returned there from captivity and about how things were going in Jerusalem.

They said to me, "Things are not going well for those who returned to the province of Judah. They are in great trouble and disgrace. The wall of Jerusalem has been torn down, and the gates have been destroyed by fire."

When I heard this, I sat down and wept. In fact, for days I mourned, fasted, and prayed to the God of heaven. Then I said,

"O LORD, God of heaven, the great and awesome God who keeps his covenant of unfailing love with those who love him and obey his commands, listen to my prayer! Look down and see me praying night and day for your people Israel. I confess that we have sinned against you. Yes, even my own family and I have sinned! We have sinned terribly by not obeying the commands, decrees, and regulations that you gave us through your servant Moses.

"Please remember what you told your servant Moses: 'If you are unfaithful to me, I will scatter you among the nations. But if you return to me and obey my commands and live by them, then even if you are exiled to the ends of the earth, I will bring you back to the place I have chosen for my name to be honored.'

"The people you rescued by your great power and strong hand are your servants. O Lord, please hear my prayer! Listen to the prayers of those of us who delight in honoring you. Please grant me success today by making the king favorable to me. Put it into his heart to be kind to me."

In those days I was the king's cup-bearer.

*In decision-making, prayer
precedes action.*

THE PRAYER AND
THE CHAIN SAWS

I respect my Aunt Gladys's intrepid spirit, although it concerns me sometimes. Once, the source of my concern came in the form of an email: "I cut down a walnut tree yesterday."

My chain saw–wielding aunt is seventy-six years old! The tree had grown up behind her garage. When the roots threatened to burst through the concrete, it had to go. But she did tell us, "I always pray before I tackle a job like that."

While serving as cup-bearer to the king of Persia during the time of Israel's exile, Nehemiah heard news concerning the people who had returned to Jerusalem: "The wall of Jerusalem is broken down, and its gates have been burned with fire" (Nehemiah 1:3). Jerusalem was vulnerable to attack by enemies. Nehemiah wanted to get involved. But prayer came first, especially since a new king had intervened to stop the building efforts in Jerusalem (see Ezra 4). Nehemiah prayed for his people (Nehemiah 1:5–10), and then he asked God for help before requesting permission from the king to leave (v. 11).

Is prayer your response? It's always the best way to face any task or trial in life.

Linda Washington

O Lord, please hear my prayer!

—NEHEMIAH 1:11 NLT

Write

Nehemiah used his unique position as the king's cup-bearer to intervene on behalf of his people. Identify a situation where you might be able to lend your help, connections, and expertise.

Connect

Adapt Nehemiah's prayer into your own, confessing your sins and asking for God's favor in whatever tasks, responsibilities, or challenges lie ahead.

> O Lord, God of heaven, the great and awesome God who keeps his covenant of unfailing love with those who love him and obey his commands, listen to my prayer! Look down and see me praying night and day for your people Israel. I confess that we have sinned against you. Yes, even my own family and I have sinned! We have sinned terribly by not obeying the commands, decrees, and regulations that you gave us through your servant Moses. . . .
>
> The people you rescued by your great power and strong hand are your servants. O Lord, please hear my prayer! Listen to the prayers of those of us who delight in honoring you. Please grant me success today by making the king favorable to me. Put it into his heart to be kind to me. (Nehemiah 1:5–7, 10–11 NLT)

Pray

Relying on God's wisdom and guidance, pray on behalf of a circumstance, person, or decision-making process.

PSALM 42 ESV

As a deer pants for flowing streams,
    so pants my soul for you, O
        God.
My soul thirsts for God,
    for the living God.
When shall I come and appear
        before God?
My tears have been my food
    day and night,
while they say to me all day long,
    "Where is your God?"
These things I remember,
    as I pour out my soul:
how I would go with the throng
    and lead them in procession to
        the house of God
with glad shouts and songs of praise
    a multitude keeping festival.

Why are you cast down, O my soul,
    and why are you in turmoil
        within me?
Hope in God; for I shall again
        praise him,
    my salvation and my God.

My soul is cast down within me;
    therefore I will remember you
from the land of the Jordan and of
        Hermon,

from Mount Mizar.
Deep calls to deep
    at the roar of your waterfalls;
all your breakers and your waves
    have gone over me.
By day the LORD commands his
        steadfast love,
    and at night his song is with me,
    a prayer to the God of my life.
I say to God, my rock:
    "Why have you forgotten me?
Why do I go about mourning
    because of the oppression of the
        enemy?"
As with a deadly wound in my
        bones,
    my adversaries taunt me,
while they say to me all the day
        long,
    "Where is your God?"

Why are you cast down, O my soul,
    and why are you in turmoil
        within me?
Hope in God; for I shall again
        praise him,
    my salvation and my God.

God can handle my
questions and fears.

A SONG IN THE NIGHT

*m*y father's life was one of longing. He longed for whole-
ness, even as Parkinson's disease gradually crippled his
mind and body. He longed for peace but was tormented by the
deep pain of depression. He longed to feel loved and cherished
but often felt utterly alone.

He found himself less alone when he read Psalm 42, his favorite psalm. Like him, the psalmist knew a desperate longing
for healing (vv. 1–2). And the psalmist knew a sadness that
seemed to never go away (v. 3), robbing him of times of pure
joy (v. 6). Like my dad, the psalmist felt abandoned by God and
asked, "Why?" (v. 9).

As the words of the psalm washed over him, assuring him he
was not alone, Dad sensed the beginnings of a quiet peace. A
tender voice surrounded him—assuring him that although the
waves still crashed over him, he was dearly loved (v. 8).

Hearing that quiet song of love was enough. Enough for my
dad to quietly cling to glimmers of hope, love, and joy. And
enough for him to wait patiently for the day his longings would
finally be satisfied (vv. 5, 11).

Monica La Rose

Connect

Slowly reread the excerpts from Psalm 42. Which verse comforts, invites, or challenges you? Write it down, allowing the Scripture to sink deeply into your heart.

> As a deer pants for flowing
> streams,
>   so pants my soul for you, O
>   God.
> My soul thirsts for God,
>   for the living God. . . .
>
> Why are you cast down, O my
>   soul,
>   and why are you in turmoil
>   within me?
> Hope in God; for I shall again
>   praise him,
>   my salvation and my God. . . .
>
> Deep calls to deep
>   at the roar of your waterfalls;
> all your breakers and your waves
>   have gone over me.
> By day the LORD commands his
>   steadfast love,
>   and at night his song is with me,
>   a prayer to the God of my life.
>   Psalm 42: 1–2, 5, 7–8 ESV

Pray

Identify a time you felt abandoned by God, as the psalmist did (v. 9). Talk with God about it.

Write

What questions or fears do you want to bring to God?

If we hope for what we do not yet have, we wait for it patiently. —ROMANS 8:25

JOB 2:7–13

So Satan went out from the presence of the Lord and afflicted Job with painful sores from the soles of his feet to the crown of his head. Then Job took a piece of broken pottery and scraped himself with it as he sat among the ashes.

His wife said to him, "Are you still maintaining your integrity? Curse God and die!"

He replied, "You are talking like a foolish woman. Shall we accept good from God, and not trouble?"

In all this, Job did not sin in what he said.

When Job's three friends, Eliphaz the Temanite, Bildad the Shuhite and Zophar the Naamathite, heard about all the troubles that had come upon him, they set out from their homes and met together by agreement to go and sympathize with him and comfort him. When they saw him from a distance, they could hardly recognize him; they began to weep aloud, and they tore their robes and sprinkled dust on their heads. Then they sat on the ground with him for seven days and seven nights. No one said a word to him, because they saw how great his suffering was.

> Being present can be a gift
> for someone hurting.

A FRIEND'S COMFORT

A mom was surprised to see her daughter muddy from the waist down when she walked in the door after school. Her daughter explained that a friend had fallen into a mud puddle. While a classmate ran to get help, the little girl felt sorry for her friend. So she went over and sat in the mud puddle with her friend until a teacher arrived.

When Job experienced the devastating loss of his children and became afflicted with painful sores on his entire body, his suffering was overwhelming. Three of his friends wanted to comfort him. "They began to weep aloud, and they tore their robes and sprinkled dust on their heads. Then they sat on the ground with him for seven days and seven nights. No one said a word to him, because they saw how great his suffering was" (Job 2:12–13).

Job's friends initially showed remarkable understanding. Although they later gave Job some poor advice, their first response was good because it showed true empathy.

Often the best thing we can do when comforting a hurting friend is to sit with them in their suffering.

Lisa M. Samra

Write

Following the loss of a loved one, in Jewish tradition, the family of the deceased sits together for seven days to grieve. A time to mourn and not worry about anything else . . . they don't even prepare their own food. It's called sitting shiva. Friends of the family pay shiva calls to offer assistance to the family. What ways could you offer support or pay a shiva call to a struggling friend or loved one?

No one said a word to him, because they saw how great his suffering was.

—JOB 2:13

Connect

Take a few minutes to pray for a friend, acquaintance, or family member who is struggling. Ask the Holy Spirit to show you how to best intercede for them.

Pray

Identify someone whose actions encouraged you during a challenging season or circumstance. Thank God for them.

DANIEL 10:1–14 ESV

In the third year of Cyrus king of Persia a word was revealed to Daniel, who was named Belteshazzar. And the word was true, and it was a great conflict. And he understood the word and had understanding of the vision.

In those days I, Daniel, was mourning for three weeks. I ate no delicacies, no meat or wine entered my mouth, nor did I anoint myself at all, for the full three weeks. On the twenty-fourth day of the first month, as I was standing on the bank of the great river (that is, the Tigris) I lifted up my eyes and looked, and behold, a man clothed in linen, with a belt of fine gold from Uphaz around his waist. His body was like beryl, his face like the appearance of lightning, his eyes like flaming torches, his arms and legs like the gleam of burnished bronze, and the sound of his words like the sound of a multitude. And I, Daniel, alone saw the vision, for the men who were with me did not see the vision, but a great trembling fell upon them, and they fled to hide themselves. So I was left alone and saw this great vision, and no strength was left in me. My radiant appearance was fearfully changed, and I retained no strength. Then I heard the sound of his words, and as I heard the sound of his words, I fell on my face in deep sleep with my face to the ground.

And behold, a hand touched me and set me trembling on my hands and knees. And he said to me, "O Daniel, man greatly loved, understand the words that I speak to you, and stand upright, for now I have been sent to you." And when he had spoken this word to me, I stood up trembling. Then he said to me, "Fear not, Daniel, for from the first day that you set your heart to understand and humbled yourself before your God, your words have been heard, and I have come because of your words. The prince of the kingdom of Persia withstood me twenty-one days, but Michael, one of the chief princes, came to help me, for I was left there with the kings of Persia, and came to make you understand what is to happen to your people in the latter days. For the vision is for days yet to come."

God is at work, even
when it's invisible.

· ·

BEHIND THE SCENES

*M*y daughter texted a friend, hoping to have a question answered quickly. Her phone indicated that the recipient had read the message, so she waited anxiously. Mere moments passed, yet she grew frustrated at the delay. Irritation eroded into worry; she wondered whether there might be a problem between them. Eventually a reply came, and my daughter was relieved that their relationship was fine. Her friend had simply been seeking an answer.

The prophet Daniel also anxiously awaited a reply. After receiving a frightening vision, Daniel fasted and sought God through prayer (10:3, 12). Finally, after three weeks (vv. 2, 13), an angel arrived and assured Daniel his prayers had been heard since the first day, and he had been battling on behalf of those prayers. God was at work during each of the twenty-one days that elapsed between Daniel's first prayer and the angel's coming.

We can grow anxious when God's reply doesn't come when we want it to. We're prone to wonder whether He cares. Yet Daniel's experience reminds us that God is at work on behalf of those He loves even when it isn't obvious to us.

Kirsten Holmberg

Pray

Talk to God about an unanswered prayer.

Connect

In what area of your life would you like God's help, direction, or wisdom? Ask Jesus for what you need, listening for His loving guidance.

Write

When was a time you had to wait on God to answer your prayers? How did (or does) that feel?

[The angel said,]
"Your words
have been heard,
and I have
come because
of your words."
—DANIEL 10:12 ESV

MATTHEW 6:1–4

Be careful not to practice your righteousness in front of others to be seen by them. If you do, you will have no reward from your Father in heaven.

So when you give to the needy, do not announce it with trumpets, as the hypocrites do in the synagogues and on the streets, to be honored by others. Truly I tell you, they have received their reward in full. But when you give to the needy, do not let your left hand know what your right hand is doing, so that your giving may be in secret. Then your Father, who sees what is done in secret, will reward you.

God sees—and receives
the glory—when I give.

ANONYMOUS KINDNESS

When I first graduated from college, I adopted a strict grocery budget—twenty-five dollars a week. One day at the grocery store, I suspected my items cost slightly more than my remaining money. "Stop when we reach twenty dollars," I told the cashier, and I was able to purchase everything I'd selected but a bag of peppers.

As I was about to drive home, a man stopped by my car. "Here's your peppers, ma'am," he said, handing the bag to me. Before I had time to thank him, he was already walking away.

The simple goodness of this kind act brings to mind Jesus's words in Matthew 6. Criticizing those who made a show of giving to the needy (v. 2), Jesus taught His disciples a different way. He urged that giving should be done so secretly it's like the left hand isn't even aware the right is giving (v. 3)!

Giving should never be about us. We give because of what our generous God has so lavishly given us (2 Corinthians 9:6–11). As we give quietly and generously, we reflect who He is—and God receives the thanksgiving (v. 11).

Monica La Rose

When you give to the needy, do not let your left hand know what your right hand is doing. —MATTHEW 6:3

Write

When have you received anonymous kindness from someone?

Connect

James 1:17 says, "Every good and perfect gift is from above, coming down from the Father of the heavenly lights, who does not change like shifting shadows." Since we serve a generous God, what would you like to tell Him or ask Him?

Pray

Ask God if there is a unique or creative way He'd like for you to give or serve in this season.

ISAIAH 55:1–7

"Come, all you who are thirsty,
    come to the waters;
and you who have no money,
    come, buy and eat!
Come, buy wine and milk
    without money and without cost.
Why spend money on what is not bread,
    and your labor on what does not satisfy?
Listen, listen to me, and eat what is good,
    and you will delight in the richest of fare.
Give ear and come to me;
    listen, that you may live.
I will make an everlasting covenant with you,
    my faithful love promised to David.
See, I have made him a witness to the peoples,
    a ruler and commander of the peoples.
Surely you will summon nations you know not,
    and nations you do not know will come running to
            you,
because of the Lord your God,
    the Holy One of Israel,
    for he has endowed you with splendor."

Seek the Lord while he may be found;
    call on him while he is near.
Let the wicked forsake their ways
    and the unrighteous their thoughts.
Let them turn to the Lord, and he will have mercy
            on them,
    and to our God, for he will freely pardon.

In God's presence, I am
deeply satisfied.

THE ULTIMATE
SATISFACTION

*A*s we distributed snacks for children at a Bible school program, we noticed a little boy who devoured his snack. He also ate the leftovers of other children at his table. Even an extra bag of popcorn didn't satisfy him. We wondered why this little boy was so hungry.

It occurred to me that we can be like that boy when it comes to our emotions. We look for ways to satisfy our deepest longings, but we never find what fully satisfies us.

The prophet Isaiah invites those who hunger and thirst to "come, buy and eat" (Isaiah 55:1). Isaiah is talking about more than physical hunger. God can satisfy our spiritual and emotional hunger through the promise of His presence. The "everlasting covenant" (v. 3) is a reminder of a promise God made to David in 2 Samuel 7:8–16. Through David's family line, a Savior would come to reconnect people to God. Later, in John 6:35 and 7:37, Jesus extended the same invitation Isaiah gave, thus identifying Himself as the foretold Savior.

Hungry? God invites you to come and be filled in His presence.

Linda Washington

Connect

God offers: "Listen, listen to me, and eat what is good, and you will delight in the richest of fare" (Isaiah 55:2). For a few minutes, let yourself relax in God's presence and take joy in just spending time with your Comforter, Redeemer, and Friend. Journal about your experience.

Pray

Talk to God about your deepest desire.

Write

Where do you feel emotionally or spiritually empty?

Come, all you who are thirsty, come to the waters; and you who have no money, come, buy and eat! –ISAIAH 55:1

GENESIS 12:1–9 NLT

The LORD had said to Abram, "Leave your native country, your relatives, and your father's family, and go to the land that I will show you. I will make you into a great nation. I will bless you and make you famous, and you will be a blessing to others. I will bless those who bless you and curse those who treat you with contempt. All the families on earth will be blessed through you."

So Abram departed as the LORD had instructed, and Lot went with him. Abram was seventy-five years old when he left Haran. He took his wife, Sarai, his nephew Lot, and all his wealth—his livestock and all the people he had taken into his household at Haran—and headed for the land of Canaan. When they arrived in Canaan, Abram traveled through the land as far as Shechem. There he set up camp beside the oak of Moreh. At that time, the area was inhabited by Canaanites.

Then the LORD appeared to Abram and said, "I will give this land to your descendants." And Abram built an altar there and dedicated it to the LORD, who had appeared to him. After that, Abram traveled south and set up camp in the hill country, with Bethel to the west and Ai to the east. There he built another altar and dedicated it to the LORD, and he worshiped the LORD. Then Abram continued traveling south by stages toward the Negev.

God's plans for me
are trustworthy.

LETTING GO

For our wedding anniversary, my husband borrowed a tandem bike for a romantic adventure together. As we began to pedal on our way, I quickly realized that as the rider on the back, my vision of the road ahead was eclipsed by my husband's broad shoulders. Also, my handlebars were fixed; they didn't affect the steering of our bike. Only the front handlebars determined our direction; mine served merely as support for my upper body. I had a choice: either be frustrated by my lack of control or embrace the journey and trust Mike.

When God asked Abram to leave his homeland and family, He didn't offer much information concerning the destination. No geographic coordinates. No description of the new land or its natural resources. No indication of how long it would take to get there. God simply said, "Go." Abram's obedience to God's instruction, despite lacking the details most humans crave, is credited to him as faith (Hebrews 11:8).

If we find ourselves grappling with uncertainty or a lack of control in life, let's seek to adopt Abram's example of following and trusting God. The Lord will steer us well.

Kirsten Holmberg

Write

Where in your life are you afraid to let go of a situation or outcome? How can you entrust it to God?

The Lord had said to Abram, "Leave your native country, your relatives, and your father's family, and go to the land that I will show you."

—GENESIS 12:1 NLT

Connect

Would you describe yourself as a planner or someone who likes to go with the flow? Given your personality, how might you have responded to God's direction to "leave your native country, your relatives, and your father's family, and go to the land that I will show you" (Genesis 12:1 NLT)?

Pray

Identify an adventure God may be inviting you
to embark on. Talk with Him about it.

MARK 10:46–52

Then they came to Jericho. As Jesus and his disciples, together with a large crowd, were leaving the city, a blind man, Bartimaeus (which means "son of Timaeus"), was sitting by the roadside begging. When he heard that it was Jesus of Nazareth, he began to shout, "Jesus, Son of David, have mercy on me!"

Many rebuked him and told him to be quiet, but he shouted all the more, "Son of David, have mercy on me!"

Jesus stopped and said, "Call him."

So they called to the blind man, "Cheer up! On your feet! He's calling you." Throwing his cloak aside, he jumped to his feet and came to Jesus.

"What do you want me to do for you?" Jesus asked him.

The blind man said, "Rabbi, I want to see."

"Go," said Jesus, "your faith has healed you." Immediately he received his sight and followed Jesus along the road.

Jesus wants me to boldly ask
Him to provide for all my needs.

ASKING FOR HELP

*H*er email arrived late in a long day. Working overtime to help a family member manage his serious illness, I didn't have time for social distractions. So I didn't open it.

The next morning when I opened my friend's message, I saw this: "Can I help you in any way?" Feeling embarrassed, I started to answer no. Then I noticed that her question sounded familiar—if not divine.

That's because Jesus asked it. Hearing a blind beggar call out to Him on the Jericho Road, Jesus stopped to ask Bartimaeus a similar question: Can I help? Or as Jesus said: "What do you want me to do for you?" (Mark 10:51).

The question is stunning. It shows that the Healer, Jesus, longs to help us. But first, we're invited to admit needing Him—a humbling step. The "professional" beggar Bartimaeus simply told Jesus his most basic need: "I want to see."

It was an honest plea. Jesus healed him immediately of his basic need. Do you know your basic need today? When a friend asks, tell it. Then take your plea even higher. Tell God.

Patricia Raybon

Pray

Tell God what you want Him to do for you (Mark 10:51).

Connect

Enter into the scene of Mark 10 by imagining yourself as Bartimaeus. Feel your desperation as you say, "Jesus, Son of David, have mercy on me!" As others try to silence you, how do you feel? When Jesus asks, "What do you want me to do for you?" what is your response? What are your hopes and fears?

Write

If God were to ask you, "What do you want me to do for you?" as He did to Bartimaeus, how would you respond?

"What do you want me to do for you?" Jesus asked him.

—MARK 10:51

ESTHER 4:8-16 NLT

Mordecai gave Hathach a copy of the decree issued in Susa that called for the death of all Jews. He asked Hathach to show it to Esther and explain the situation to her. He also asked Hathach to direct her to go to the king to beg for mercy and plead for her people. So Hathach returned to Esther with Mordecai's message.

Then Esther told Hathach to go back and relay this message to Mordecai: "All the king's officials and even the people in the provinces know that anyone who appears before the king in his inner court without being invited is doomed to die unless the king holds out his gold scepter. And the king has not called for me to come to him for thirty days." So Hathach gave Esther's message to Mordecai.

Mordecai sent this reply to Esther: "Don't think for a moment that because you're in the palace you will escape when all other Jews are killed. If you keep quiet at a time like this, deliverance and relief for the Jews will arise from some other place, but you and your relatives will die. Who knows if perhaps you were made queen for just such a time as this?"

Then Esther sent this reply to Mordecai: "Go and gather together all the Jews of Susa and fast for me. Do not eat or drink for three days, night or day. My maids and I will do the same. And then, though it is against the law, I will go in to see the king. If I must die, I must die."

> May God grant me the courage
> to stand against injustice.

RIGHTEOUS AMONG THE NATIONS

At Yad Vashem, Israel's Holocaust museum, my husband and I went to the Righteous Among the Nations garden, which honors those who risked their lives to save Jewish people during the Holocaust. While looking at the memorial, we met a group from the Netherlands. One woman was there to see her grandparents' names listed on the large plaques. Intrigued, we asked about her family's story.

Members of a resistance network, the woman's grandparents Reverend Pieter and Adriana Müller took in a two-year-old Jewish boy and passed him off as the youngest of their eight children from 1943–1945.

Moved by the story, we asked, "Did the little boy survive?" An older gentleman in the group stepped forward and proclaimed, "I am that boy!"

The bravery of many to act on behalf of the Jewish people reminds me of Queen Esther. Perhaps she could have avoided death under King Xerxes's decree to annihilate the Jews around 475 bc by continuing to conceal her ethnicity. But she risked everything to confront her husband and win protection for her people.

If we are ever required to speak out against an injustice, may God grant us the courage He gave the Müllers and Queen Esther.

Lisa M. Samra

For just such a time as this.

—ESTHER 4:14 NLT

Write

Identify a time God gave you the courage to do the right thing. How did God demonstrate His faithfulness and care to you throughout the experience?

Connect

Read Esther 4, and identify a word, phrase, or part that "shimmers" for you. Write it down, and reflect on its life-giving wisdom.

Pray

Ask God where He's inviting you to be bold.

ECCLESIASTES 4:9–12

Two are better than one,
    because they have a good return for their labor:
If either of them falls down,
    one can help the other up.
But pity anyone who falls
    and has no one to help them up.
Also, if two lie down together, they will keep warm.
    But how can one keep warm alone?
Though one may be overpowered,
    two can defend themselves.
A cord of three strands is not quickly broken.

> The spiritual race is not meant to be run alone.

LET'S FINISH THE RACE

*I*n the 2016 Rio Olympics, two athletes in the 5,000-meter race caught the world's attention. About 3,200 meters into the race, New Zealander Nikki Hamblin and American Abbey D'Agostino collided and fell. Abbey was quickly up on her feet, but she stopped to help Nikki. Moments after the two athletes had started running again, Abbey began faltering, her right leg injured as a result of the fall. It was now Nikki's turn to stop and encourage her fellow athlete to finish the race. When Abbey eventually stumbled across the finish line, Nikki was waiting to embrace her. What a beautiful picture of mutual encouragement!

That sounds like Ecclesiastes 4: "Two are better than one. . . . If either of them falls down, one can help the other up" (vv. 9–10). As runners in a spiritual race, we need one another—perhaps even more so, for we are not competing. We are members of the same team.

The spiritual race is not to be run alone. Is God leading you to be a Nikki or Abbey in someone's life? Respond to His prompting today, and together let's finish the race!

Poh Fang Chia

Connect

Think about someone who has shown up for you in a time of need. Write them a thank-you letter.

Pray

Ask God to bring to mind someone who can offer you reassuring guidance or support about a decision.

Write

How might God be leading you to be a Nikki or Abbey in someone's life?

Two are better than one, because they have a good return for their labor: If either of them falls down, one can help the other up.

—ECCLESIASTES 4:9-10

JOHN 14:25–31

All this I have spoken while still with you. But the Advocate, the Holy Spirit, whom the Father will send in my name, will teach you all things and will remind you of everything I have said to you. Peace I leave with you; my peace I give you. I do not give to you as the world gives. Do not let your hearts be troubled and do not be afraid.

You heard me say, "I am going away and I am coming back to you." If you loved me, you would be glad that I am going to the Father, for the Father is greater than I. I have told you now before it happens, so that when it does happen you will believe. I will not say much more to you, for the prince of this world is coming. He has no hold over me, but he comes so that the world may learn that I love the Father and do exactly what my Father has commanded me.

Come now; let us leave.

God is for me.

CAN WE RELAX?

Darnell entered the physical therapist's office knowing he would experience a lot of pain. The therapist stretched and bent his arm and held it in positions it hadn't been in for months since his injury. After holding each uncomfortable position for a few seconds, she gently told him: "Okay, you can relax." He said later, "I think I heard that at least fifty times in each therapy session: 'Okay, you can relax.'"

Thinking of those words, Darnell realized they could apply to the rest of his life as well. He could relax in God's goodness and faithfulness instead of worrying.

As Jesus neared His death, He wanted to encourage His disciples. So He said He would send the Holy Spirit to live with them and remind them of what He had taught (John 14:26). And so, He could say, "Peace I leave with you; . . . Do not let your hearts be troubled and do not be afraid" (v. 27).

There's plenty we could be uptight about in our everyday lives. But as we draw on God's strength, we can hear Him in the therapist's words: "Okay, you can relax."

Anne Cetas

Write

Listen to Jesus's words in John 14:27: "Peace I leave with you; my peace I give you. I do not give to you as the world gives. Do not let your hearts be troubled and do not be afraid." What stands out to you about Christ's invitation here?

Do not let your hearts be troubled and do not be afraid.

—JOHN 14:27

Connect

Read the following verses on peace, then select and copy one you'd like to reflect on as you go about your day.

You will keep in perfect peace those whose minds are steadfast, because they trust in you. (Isaiah 26:3)

I have said these things to you, that in me you may have peace. In the world you will have tribulation. But take heart; I have overcome the world. (John 16:33 ESV)

Do not be anxious about anything, but in every situation, by prayer and petition, with thanksgiving, present your requests to God. And the peace of God, which transcends all understanding, will guard your hearts and your minds in Christ Jesus. (Philippians 4:6–7)

And let the peace that comes from Christ rule in your hearts. For as members of one body you are called to live in peace. And always be thankful. (Colossians 3:15 NLT)

Pray

Name a current anxiety or fear. Ask
Jesus for help with this concern.

REVELATION 22:1–5

Then the angel showed me the river of the water of life, as clear as crystal, flowing from the throne of God and of the Lamb down the middle of the great street of the city. On each side of the river stood the tree of life, bearing twelve crops of fruit, yielding its fruit every month. And the leaves of the tree are for the healing of the nations. No longer will there be any curse. The throne of God and of the Lamb will be in the city, and his servants will serve him. They will see his face, and his name will be on their foreheads. There will be no more night. They will not need the light of a lamp or the light of the sun, for the Lord God will give them light. And they will reign for ever and ever.

Knowing the end of the
story gives me hope.

A GOOD ENDING

*A*s the lights dimmed and we prepared to watch *Apollo 13*, my friend said under his breath, "Shame they all died." I watched the movie about the 1970 spaceflight with apprehension, waiting for tragedy to strike. Only near the closing credits did I realize I'd been duped. Although the astronauts faced many hardships, they made it home alive.

In Christ, we can know the end of the story—that we, too, will make it home alive. By that I mean we will live forever with our heavenly Father. The book of Revelation tells us the Lord will create a "new heaven and a new earth" (21:1). In the new city, the Lord God will welcome His people to live with Him, without fear and without the night. Knowing the end of the story gives us hope.

This can transform times of extreme difficulty, such as when people face the loss of a loved one. Although we recoil at the thought of dying, we can embrace the promise of eternity. We long for the city where we'll live forever by God's light (22:5).

Amy Boucher Pye

Pray

With God, brainstorm the sights, sounds, scents, tastes, and experiences you're looking forward to in the new heaven and earth.

Connect

While a hope-filled future awaits us, today we still live in a world of pain and suffering. In what ways are you grieving or struggling? Name and identify your disappointments, heartaches, and frustrations, then talk with God about them.

Write

What image from Revelation 22:1–5 describing the new heaven and new earth mesmerizes you?

The throne of God and of the Lamb will be in the city, and his servants will serve him. They will see his face.

—REVELATION 22:3-4

1 KINGS 17:15–24

She went away and did as Elijah had told her. So there was food every day for Elijah and for the woman and her family. For the jar of flour was not used up and the jug of oil did not run dry, in keeping with the word of the LORD spoken by Elijah.

Some time later the son of the woman who owned the house became ill. He grew worse and worse, and finally stopped breathing. She said to Elijah, "What do you have against me, man of God? Did you come to remind me of my sin and kill my son?"

"Give me your son," Elijah replied. He took him from her arms, carried him to the upper room where he was staying, and laid him on his bed. Then he cried out to the LORD, "LORD my God, have you brought tragedy even on this widow I am staying with, by causing her son to die?" Then he stretched himself out on the boy three times and cried out to the LORD, "LORD my God, let this boy's life return to him!"

The LORD heard Elijah's cry, and the boy's life returned to him, and he lived. Elijah picked up the child and carried him down from the room into the house. He gave him to his mother and said, "Look, your son is alive!"

Then the woman said to Elijah, "Now I know that you are a man of God and that the word of the LORD from your mouth is the truth."

I can rest in God's purposes for me, no matter the circumstances.

WHEN THE BOTTOM DROPS OUT

During the 1997 Asian Financial Crisis, I lost my job. After nine anxious months, I landed employment as a copywriter. But the company fell on bad times, and I was jobless again.

Ever been there? It seems like the worst is over when suddenly the bottom drops out. The widow at Zarephath could relate (1 Kings 17:12). Due to a famine, she was preparing the last meal for herself and her son when the prophet Elijah requested a bite to eat. She reluctantly agreed, and God provided a continuous supply of flour and oil (vv. 10–16).

But then her son fell ill. His health declined until he stopped breathing. The widow cried out, "What do you have against me, man of God? Did you come to remind me of my sin and kill my son?" (v. 18).

Elijah took the concern to God, praying earnestly and honestly for the boy, and God raised him up (vv. 20–22)!

When the bottom drops out, may we—like Elijah—realize that we can rest in God's purposes even as we pray for understanding. He won't desert us.

Poh Fang Chia

Let us then approach God's throne of grace with confidence, so that we may receive mercy and find grace to help us in our time of need. —HEBREWS 4:16

Write

Think about a time when the bottom dropped out in your own life. How did you feel at the time? How do you feel about the experience today?

Connect

Enter into 1 Kings 17:15–24, imagining yourself as the widow devastated by the loss of her only son. When the prophet takes the dead boy from your arms to the upper room, cry out to him. What are your expectations in this moment? Your feelings? As your son is revived, what do you do?

Pray

Talk to God about an area of your life
where you struggle to trust Him.

MATTHEW 13:53–58

When Jesus had finished these parables, he moved on from there. Coming to his hometown, he began teaching the people in their synagogue, and they were amazed. "Where did this man get this wisdom and these miraculous powers?" they asked. "Isn't this the carpenter's son? Isn't his mother's name Mary, and aren't his brothers James, Joseph, Simon and Judas? Aren't all his sisters with us? Where then did this man get all these things?" And they took offense at him.

But Jesus said to them, "A prophet is not without honor except in his own town and in his own home."

And he did not do many miracles there because of their lack of faith.

> God wants me to invite
> Him into the mundane and
> messy details of my day.

EXPECT THE MESSIAH

*T*he repairman looked young—too young to fix our problem, a car that wouldn't start. "He's just a kid," my husband, Dan, whispered to me. His disbelief sounded like the grumbling in Nazareth, where citizens doubted who Jesus was.

"Isn't this the carpenter's son?" they asked when Jesus taught in the synagogue (Matthew 13:55). Scoffing, they were surprised to hear that someone they knew was healing and teaching, and they asked, "Where did this man get this wisdom and these miraculous powers?" (v. 54). Instead of trusting in Jesus, they were offended by the authority he displayed (vv. 15, 58).

Similarly, we may struggle to trust our Savior's wisdom and power, especially in the mundane details of daily life. When we do, we may miss out on the wonder of His life transforming ours (v. 58).

The help Dan needed was right there. The young mechanic switched just one bolt and had the car running in seconds—engine humming and lights ablaze. "It lit up like Christmas," Dan said.

So too can we expect the Messiah to bring fresh light and help into our daily journey with Him.

Patricia Raybon

Connect

Describe a circumstance in which you need wisdom and guidance. Invite God to look at the situation with you, asking for clarity about the circumstance and the courage to wait expectantly on His response.

Pray

Identify an area of your life—or in the lives of those you love—in which you need a miracle. Talk to God about it.

Write

Where have you already seen God's transforming work in your life?

Isn't this the carpenter's son? Isn't his mother's name Mary? —MATTHEW 13:55

MATTHEW 13:44–46

The kingdom of heaven is like treasure hidden in a field. When a man found it, he hid it again, and then in his joy went and sold all he had and bought that field.

Again, the kingdom of heaven is like a merchant looking for fine pearls. When he found one of great value, he went away and sold everything he had and bought it.

God promises that when I
seek Him, I will find Him.

· ·

RING IN A DUMPSTER

*I*n college, I woke up one morning to find Carol, my room-
mate, in a panic. Her signet ring was missing. We searched
everywhere—even in a dumpster.

I ripped open a trash bag. "You're so dedicated to finding this!"

"I'm not losing a two-hundred-dollar ring!" she exclaimed.

Carol's determination reminds me of Jesus's parable about the
kingdom of heaven, which "is like treasure hidden in a field. When
a man found it, he hid it again, and then in his joy went and sold
all he had and bought that field" (Matthew 13:44). Certain things
are worth going to great lengths to find.

God promises that those who seek Him will find Him. In
Deuteronomy, He explained to the Israelites that they would
find Him when they turned from their sin and sought Him with
all their hearts (4:28–29). And in Jeremiah, God gave the same
promise to the exiles, saying He would bring them back from
captivity (29:13–14).

If we seek God through His Word, worship, and prayer, we
will find Him and know Him. That's even better than the sweet
moment when Carol pulled her ring out of a trash bag!

Julie Schwab

Write

Have you ever gone to great lengths to pursue something or someone? What was that experience like?

Seek and you will find; knock and the door will be opened to you.

—MATTHEW 7:7

Connect

God promises that "you will seek me and find me when you seek me with all your heart" (Jeremiah 29:13). Ask Jesus about fresh ways to seek Him and His ways in this season.

Pray

Allow God to share His dreams and desires for you.

1 SAMUEL 25:14–25

One of the servants told Abigail, Nabal's wife, "David sent messengers from the wilderness to give our master his greetings, but he hurled insults at them. Yet these men were very good to us. They did not mistreat us, and the whole time we were out in the fields near them nothing was missing. Night and day they were a wall around us the whole time we were herding our sheep near them. Now think it over and see what you can do, because disaster is hanging over our master and his whole household. He is such a wicked man that no one can talk to him."

Abigail acted quickly. She took two hundred loaves of bread, two skins of wine, five dressed sheep, five seahs of roasted grain, a hundred cakes of raisins and two hundred cakes of pressed figs, and loaded them on donkeys. Then she told her servants, "Go on ahead; I'll follow you." But she did not tell her husband Nabal.

As she came riding her donkey into a mountain ravine, there were David and his men descending toward her, and she met them. David had just said, "It's been useless—all my watching over this fellow's property in the wilderness so that nothing of his was missing. He has paid me back evil for good. May God deal with David, be it ever so severely, if by morning I leave alive one male of all who belong to him!"

When Abigail saw David, she quickly got off her donkey and bowed down before David with her face to the ground. She fell at his feet and said: "Pardon your servant, my lord, and let me speak to you; hear what your servant has to say. Please pay no attention, my lord, to that wicked man Nabal. He is just like his name—his name means Fool, and folly goes with him. And as for me, your servant, I did not see the men my lord sent."

God equips me for hard
conversations.

HARD CONVERSATIONS

I once drove fifty miles to have a hard conversation with a remote staff person who had been presenting our company improperly to others.

In 1 Samuel 25, a woman named Abigail took great personal risk to confront a future king of Israel about a disastrous choice he was about to make. Abigail was married to Nabal, whose character matched the meaning of his name ("fool"; vv. 3, 25). Nabal had refused to pay David and his troops the customary wage for protecting his livestock (vv. 10–11). Hearing that David planned a murderous revenge on her household and knowing her foolish husband wouldn't listen to reason, Abigail prepared a peace offering, rode to meet David, and persuaded him to reconsider (vv. 18–31).

How did Abigail accomplish this? She spoke truth to David, reminding him of God's call on his life. If he resisted his desire for revenge, when God made him king, he wouldn't "have on his conscience the staggering burden of needless bloodshed" (v. 31).

You might know someone dangerously close to making a harmful mistake. Like Abigail, might God be calling you to a hard conversation?

Elisa Morgan

Pray

Name a healthy or unhealthy relationship in your life. Ask for God's perspective on the relationship.

Connect

Make a list of the significant relationships in your life. Next to each name recorded, identify what you treasure about the person and value about the relationship.

Write

As you read 1 Samuel 25:14–19, what stands out to you about how Abigail managed a crisis?

If it is possible, as far as it depends on you, live at peace with everyone.

—ROMANS 12:18

1 KINGS 19:19–21

So Elijah went from there and found Elisha son of Shaphat. He was plowing with twelve yoke of oxen, and he himself was driving the twelfth pair. Elijah went up to him and threw his cloak around him. Elisha then left his oxen and ran after Elijah. "Let me kiss my father and mother goodbye," he said, "and then I will come with you."

"Go back," Elijah replied. "What have I done to you?"

So Elisha left him and went back. He took his yoke of oxen and slaughtered them. He burned the plowing equipment to cook the meat and gave it to the people, and they ate. Then he set out to follow Elijah and became his servant.

*I will follow Jesus,
whatever the cost.*

FOLLOWING
WHERE HE LEADS

s a child, I looked forward to our church's Sunday evening services. They were exciting. Sunday night often meant we got to hear from missionaries and other guest speakers. Their messages inspired me because of their willingness to leave family and friends—and, at times, homes, possessions, and careers—to go off to strange, unfamiliar, and sometimes dangerous places to serve God.

Like those missionaries, Elisha left many things behind to follow God (1 Kings 19:19–21). When God called him into service through Elijah, he was a farmer. The prophet Elijah met him in the field where he was plowing, threw his cloak over Elisha's shoulders (the symbol of his role as prophet), and called him to follow. After giving his mother a kiss and saying goodbye to his father, Elisha sacrificed his oxen, burned his plowing equipment, and followed Elijah.

God wants all of us to follow Him and to "live as a believer in whatever situation the Lord has assigned to [us], just as God has called [us]" (1 Corinthians 7:17). Serving God can be thrilling and challenging no matter where we are—even if we never leave home.

Alyson Kieda

*Then [Elisha] set out to follow Elijah
and became his servant.* —1 KINGS 19:21

Write

Before Elisha became a prophet, he was a farmer and lived faithfully. Describe the gifts, relationships, and circumstances that have shaped your character.

Connect

Enter into the story of 1 Kings 19:19–21 by imagining yourself as Elisha. When the prophet Elijah throws his cloak around you to name you as his successor, what are your hopes, fears, and expectations? At this crossroads in your life, how will you respond? What do you want to do?

Pray

Where in your life are you feeling drawn to something new? Talk to God about it.

JOHN 20:11–18 ESV

Mary stood weeping outside the tomb, and as she wept she stooped to look into the tomb. And she saw two angels in white, sitting where the body of Jesus had lain, one at the head and one at the feet. They said to her, "Woman, why are you weeping?" She said to them, "They have taken away my Lord, and I do not know where they have laid him." Having said this, she turned around and saw Jesus standing, but she did not know that it was Jesus. Jesus said to her, "Woman, why are you weeping? Whom are you seeking?" Supposing him to be the gardener, she said to him, "Sir, if you have carried him away, tell me where you have laid him, and I will take him away." Jesus said to her, "Mary." She turned and said to him in Aramaic, "Rabboni!" (which means Teacher). Jesus said to her, "Do not cling to me, for I have not yet ascended to the Father; but go to my brothers and say to them, 'I am ascending to my Father and your Father, to my God and your God.'" Mary Magdalene went and announced to the disciples, "I have seen the Lord"—and that he had said these things to her.

CALLED BY NAME

*A*dvertisers have concluded that the most attention-grabbing word that viewers react to is their own name. Thus, a television channel in the UK introduced personalized advertisements with their online streaming services.

Even more than that, there's a closeness that comes when someone who loves us says our name. Mary Magdalene's attention was arrested when, at the tomb where Jesus's body had been laid after He was crucified on the cross, He spoke her name (John 20:16). With that single word, she turned in recognition to the Teacher she loved, and she followed Him. The familiarity with which He spoke her name confirmed for her that the One who'd known her perfectly was alive.

Like Mary, we too are personally loved by God. Jesus told Mary that He would ascend to His Father (v. 17), but He had also told His disciples that He would not leave them alone (John 14:15–18). God would send the Holy Spirit to live and dwell in His children (Acts 2:1–13).

God's story doesn't change. Whether then or now, He knows those He loves (see John 10:14–15). He calls us by name.

Amy Boucher Pye

Connect

Imagine standing before Jesus, as Mary did in John 20. Hear Jesus say your name, as only your Savior who loves you more than anyone else can say it. What is Jesus's expression toward you? How do you respond to Him?

Pray

Identify how God has been growing your faith lately, and have a conversation with Him about it.

Write

Read the excerpt from John 20, reviewing the dialogue. Does a question or comment from the dialogue stand out to you? Sit with that question or phrase, and journal your response to it.

> [The angels] said to her, "Woman, why are you weeping?" She said to them, "They have taken away my Lord, and I do not know where they have laid him." Having said this, she turned around and saw Jesus standing, but she did not know that it was Jesus. Jesus said to her, "Woman, why are you weeping? Whom are you seeking?" Supposing him to be the gardener, she said to him, "Sir, if you have carried him away, tell me where you have laid him, and I will take him away." Jesus said to her, "Mary." She turned and said to him in Aramaic, "Rabboni!" (John 20:13–16 ESV)

Jesus said to her, "Mary." She turned and said to him in Aramaic, "Rabboni!"

—JOHN 20:16 ESV

JOSHUA 10:6–15

The Gibeonites then sent word to Joshua in the camp at Gilgal: "Do not abandon your servants. Come up to us quickly and save us! Help us, because all the Amorite kings from the hill country have joined forces against us."

So Joshua marched up from Gilgal with his entire army, including all the best fighting men. The Lord said to Joshua, "Do not be afraid of them; I have given them into your hand. Not one of them will be able to withstand you."

After an all-night march from Gilgal, Joshua took them by surprise. The Lord threw them into confusion before Israel, so Joshua and the Israelites defeated them completely at Gibeon. Israel pursued them along the road going up to Beth Horon and cut them down all the way to Azekah and Makkedah. As they fled before Israel on the road down from Beth Horon to Azekah, the Lord hurled large hailstones down on them, and more of them died from the hail than were killed by the swords of the Israelites.

On the day the Lord gave the Amorites over to Israel, Joshua said to the Lord in the presence of Israel:

> "Sun, stand still over Gibeon,
>   and you, moon, over the Valley of Aijalon."
> So the sun stood still,
>   and the moon stopped,
>   till the nation avenged itself on its enemies,

as it is written in the Book of Jashar.

The sun stopped in the middle of the sky and delayed going down about a full day. There has never been a day like it before or since, a day when the Lord listened to a human being. Surely the Lord was fighting for Israel!

Then Joshua returned with all Israel to the camp at Gilgal.

With God, all things are possible.

HELP FROM HEAVEN

The Morse code signal SOS was created in 1905 because sailors needed a way to indicate extreme distress. The signal gained renown in 1910 when used by the sinking steamship Kentucky, saving all forty-six people aboard.

While SOS may be a relatively recent invention, the urgent cry for help is as old as humanity. We hear it often in the Old Testament story of Joshua, who faced opposition from fellow Israelites (Joshua 9:18) and challenging terrain (3:15–17) as the Israelites conquered and settled the land God had promised them. During this struggle, "the LORD was with Joshua" (6:27).

In Joshua 10, the Israelites went to the aid of the Gibeonites, who were being attacked by five kings. Joshua knew he needed the Lord's help (v. 12). God responded with a hailstorm, even stopping the sun briefly to give Israel more time to defeat the enemy. Joshua 10:14 recounts, "Surely the LORD was fighting for Israel!"

Are you in the midst of a challenging situation? Send out an SOS to God. Be encouraged that God will respond to your call for help in the way that is best for His glory.

Lisa M. Samra

Write

Identify one way God has fought for you, and take time to express your gratitude.

*Surely the L*ORD *was fighting for Israel!* —JOSHUA 10:14

Connect

Listen to God's words of hope and encouragement for Joshua, and pray with one (or more) of the verses:

> I will be with you; I will never leave you nor forsake you. (Joshua 1:5)

> Do not turn from it to the right or to the left, that you may be successful wherever you go. Keep this Book of the Law always on your lips; meditate on it day and night, so that you may be careful to do everything written in it. Then you will be prosperous and successful. (Joshua 1:7–8)

> Have I not commanded you? Be strong and courageous. Do not be afraid; do not be discouraged, for the LORD your God will be with you wherever you go. (Joshua 1:9)

> Do not be afraid of them; I have given them into your hand. Not one of them will be able to withstand you. (Joshua 10:8)

Pray

Are you in the midst of a fearful or impossible situation? Cry out to God for help and deliverance, trusting that Jesus cares for you.

JOB 1:13–22

One day when Job's sons and daughters were feasting and drinking wine at the oldest brother's house, a messenger came to Job and said, "The oxen were plowing and the donkeys were grazing nearby, and the Sabeans attacked and made off with them. They put the servants to the sword, and I am the only one who has escaped to tell you!"

While he was still speaking, another messenger came and said, "The fire of God fell from the heavens and burned up the sheep and the servants, and I am the only one who has escaped to tell you!"

While he was still speaking, another messenger came and said, "The Chaldeans formed three raiding parties and swept down on your camels and made off with them. They put the servants to the sword, and I am the only one who has escaped to tell you!"

While he was still speaking, yet another messenger came and said, "Your sons and daughters were feasting and drinking wine at the oldest brother's house, when suddenly a mighty wind swept in from the desert and struck the four corners of the house. It collapsed on them and they are dead, and I am the only one who has escaped to tell you!"

At this, Job got up and tore his robe and shaved his head. Then he fell to the ground in worship and said:

> "Naked I came from my mother's womb,
>   and naked I will depart.
> The Lord gave and the Lord has taken away;
>   may the name of the Lord be praised."

In all this, Job did not sin by charging God with wrongdoing.

*God is still present and good,
whatever my struggles.*

PRAISING THROUGH PROBLEMS

"*I*t's cancer." I wanted to be strong when Mom said those words to me. But I burst into tears. You never want to hear those words even one time. But this was Mom's third bout with cancer. This time it was a malignant tumor under her arm.

Though Mom was the one with bad news, she had to comfort me. Her response was eye-opening for me: "I know God is always good to me. He's always faithful." Even as she faced a difficult surgery followed up by radiation treatments, Mom was assured of God's presence and faithfulness.

How like Job. Job lost his children, his wealth, and his health. But after hearing the news, "he fell to the ground in worship" (1:20). When advised to curse God, he said, "Shall we accept good from God, and not trouble?" (2:10). What a radical initial response! Ultimately, Job realized that God was still with him and that He still cared.

For most of us, praise is not our first response to difficulties. But watching Mom's response reminded me that God is still present, still good. He will help us through hard times.

Linda Washington

Pray

Listen to a favorite song or genre of music,
allowing it to move you to worship.
Experience God's delight in your praise.

Connect

Job never learned why God allowed His suffering or what Satan's role was in
the devastation. What struggles in your own life have left you disoriented and
fearing that God isn't good, loving, or just? Write these down, then share with
God about the experiences.

Write

What does it look like to accept good and bad from God? How can you come before Him honestly with your grief and struggles?

Shall we accept good from God, and not trouble?

—JOB 2:10

PSALM 50:8–15

I bring no charges against you concerning your
    sacrifices
  or concerning your burnt offerings, which are ever
    before me.
I have no need of a bull from your stall
  or of goats from your pens,
for every animal of the forest is mine,
  and the cattle on a thousand hills.
I know every bird in the mountains,
  and the insects in the fields are mine.
If I were hungry I would not tell you,
  for the world is mine, and all that is in it.
Do I eat the flesh of bulls
  or drink the blood of goats?

"Sacrifice thank offerings to God,
  fulfill your vows to the Most High,
and call on me in the day of trouble;
  I will deliver you, and you will honor me."

Gratitude moves God's heart.

HONORING GOD WITH THANKS

The doctor wasn't frowning, despite talking to my husband about his recent cancer diagnosis. Smiling, she offered a suggestion: start each day by giving thanks for at least three things.

Dan agreed, knowing that gratitude opens our hearts to find encouragement in God's goodness. Thus, Dan starts each day with words of praise. Thank you, God, for a good night's sleep. For my clean bed. For sunshine. For breakfast on the table. For a smile on my lips.

Does our praise in life's small details matter to Almighty God? In Psalm 50, Asaph offers a clear answer. God has "no need of a bull from your stall or of goats from your pens" (v. 9). Instead, God wants His people to give Him their hearts and lives in gratitude (vv. 14, 23), which helps our spirits flourish.

When we call on the Lord when trouble comes, He will deliver us (v. 15).

Does this mean Dan will be healed? We don't know. But for now, Dan delights in showing God he's grateful for His love and for who God is: Redeemer. Healer. Friend. And friends delight to hear this: Thank you.

Patricia Raybon

Call on me in the day of trouble; I will deliver you, and you will honor me.

—PSALM 50:15

Write

What circumstances, responsibilities, and relationships are life-giving to you? Which are draining your energy? Journal about them.

Connect

Choose a verse that stands out to you from Psalm 103 and adapt it into a prayer of gratitude to God.

> Praise the LORD, my soul;
>   all my inmost being, praise his holy name.
> Praise the LORD, my soul,
>   and forget not all his benefits—
> who forgives all your sins
>   and heals all your diseases,
> who redeems your life from the pit
>   and crowns you with love and compassion,
> who satisfies your desires with good things
>   so that your youth is renewed like the eagle's. . . .
>
> For as high as the heavens are above the earth,
>   so great is his love for those who fear him;
> as far as the east is from the west,
>   so far has he removed our transgressions from us.
>
> As a father has compassion on his children,
>   so the LORD has compassion on those who fear him;
> for he knows how we are formed,
>   he remembers that we are dust.
>
> Psalm 103:1–5; 11–14

Pray

Thank God for three gifts in your life,
and listen for His response.

LUKE 15:1–7 NLT

Tax collectors and other notorious sinners often came to listen to Jesus teach. This made the Pharisees and teachers of religious law complain that he was associating with such sinful people—even eating with them!

So Jesus told them this story: "If a man has a hundred sheep and one of them gets lost, what will he do? Won't he leave the ninety-nine others in the wilderness and go to search for the one that is lost until he finds it? And when he has found it, he will joyfully carry it home on his shoulders. When he arrives, he will call together his friends and neighbors, saying, 'Rejoice with me because I have found my lost sheep.' In the same way, there is more joy in heaven over one lost sinner who repents and returns to God than over ninety-nine others who are righteous and haven't strayed away!"

LOVE WON'T STOP

After turning nineteen (pre-cell phone era), I moved more than seven hundred miles away from my mom. One morning, I left early to run errands, forgetting our scheduled call. Later that night, two policemen came to my door. Mom had been worried because I'd never missed one of our chats. After calling repeatedly and getting a busy signal, she reached out to the authorities. One of the officers said, "It's a blessing to know love won't stop looking for you."

Later, I realized I had accidentally left the receiver off its base. After I called Mom to apologize, she said she needed to spread the good news to everyone that I was okay. I think she overreacted a bit, though it felt good to be loved that much.

Scripture paints a beautiful picture of God, who is Love, relentlessly beckoning His wandering children. Like a good shepherd, He seeks out every lost sheep, affirming the priceless value of each beloved child of God (Luke 15:1–7).

Love never stops looking for us. And we can pray for others who need to know that Love. God never stops looking for them either.

Xochitl Dixon

Connect

Luke 15 depicts God as a loving shepherd. Choose one of the Scripture passages describing God as the good shepherd and journal about it. What does the passage say about God's love for you?

> The LORD is my shepherd, I lack nothing. (Psalm 23:1)

> He [heavenly Father] tends his flock like a shepherd: He gathers the lambs in his arms and carries them close to his heart; he gently leads those that have young. (Isaiah 40:11)

> I am the good shepherd. The good shepherd lays down his life for the sheep. (John 10:11)

> My sheep listen to my voice; I know them, and they follow me. I give them eternal life, and they shall never perish; no one will snatch them out of my hand. (John 10:27–28)

Pray

Tell Jesus you're thankful that He will never stop pursuing you in love.

Write

As you conclude this forty-day devotional journey, reflect on how you have drawn closer to God. How have you learned more about His relentless, redeeming love? What would you like God to know about your experience?

Rejoice with me because I have found my lost sheep. —LUKE 15:6 NLT

CONTRIBUTORS

To learn more about the writers of *Our Daily Bread,*
visit odb.org/all-authors.

Amy Boucher Pye

Anne Cetas

Poh Fang Chia

Xochitl Dixon

Kirsten Holmberg

Alyson Kieda

Monica La Rose

Elisa Morgan

Keila Ochoa

Patricia Raybon

Lisa M. Samra

Julie Schwab

Linda Washington

Anna Haggard, General Editor, is associate content editor for Our Daily Bread Publishing. A follower of Jesus, she loves to write and edit books sharing about God's generous, deep love for all people. Anna coauthored the Called and Courageous Girls series, and she lives in Lancaster, Pennsylvania.

GOD HEARS HER

Seek and she will find

Spread the Word
by Doing One Thing.

- Give a copy of this book as a gift.
- Share the QR code link via your social media.
- Write a review of this book on your blog, favorite bookseller's website, or at ODB.org/store.
- Recommend this book to your church, small group, or book club.

Connect with us. [f] [o]
Our Daily Bread Publishing
PO Box 3566, Grand Rapids, MI 49501, USA
Email: books@odb.org

Love God. Love Others.
with  Our Daily Bread.

Your gift changes lives.

Connect with us. [f] [○]

Our Daily Bread Publishing
PO Box 3566, Grand Rapids, MI 49501, USA
Email: books@odb.org